SPEECH
& DEBATE

BOOKS BY STEPHEN KARAM PUBLISHED BY TCG

The Humans

Speech & Debate

The Cherry Orchard (forthcoming)
  By Anton Chekhov, new version by Stephen Karam

SPEECH & DEBATE

Stephen Karam

THEATRE COMMUNICATIONS GROUP
NEW YORK
2017

Speech & Debate is published by Theatre Communications Group, Inc., 520 Eighth Avenue, 24th Floor, New York, NY 10018-4156

The publication of *Speech & Debate* by Stephen Karam, through TCG's Book Program, is made possible in part by the New York State Council on the Arts with the support of Governor Andrew Cuomo and the New York State Legislature.

TCG books are exclusively distributed to the book trade by Consortium Book Sales and Distribution.

ISBN 978-1-55936-544-4 (print) / ISBN 978-1-55936-865-0 (ebook)
A catalog record for this book is available from the Library of Congress.

Book design and composition by Lisa Govan

Cover design based on the original poster art by Kevin Wolfe for American Theater Company

First Edition, June 2017

ACKNOWLEDGMENTS

This play was born out of the generous dramaturgical/creative support and talents of many people: Lowry Marshall for agreeing to workshop the play before I even finished it; Sarah Coogan, Anne Reilly, Patricia McGregor, Will Rogers, Chris Burney, Jason Moore; all of the actors listed in the first two productions; Eleanor Langan and Agnes Cummings for their Scranton High School Speech and Debate coaching genius; Robyn Goodman for believing in the piece and making it happen; Chris Till for setting everything in motion; Darius, Kerry, and Sam for introducing me to the great state of Oregon; all the folks at Roundabout: Julia Levy, Harold Wolpert, Rebecca Habel, Jill Rafson, Josh Fiedler; and Todd Haimes, for his generous and enthusiastic support throughout the entire process.

Special thanks to Mary Rodgers, Bill Gaden, and all the good people at the Rodgers & Hammerstein Organization for seeing the play and not shutting it down. All S & D vocals are now and forever for you, Mary.

SPEECH
& DEBATE

Speech & Debate was first performed as a workshop production at Brown/Trinity Playwrights Repertory Theatre (Lowry Marshall, Artistic Director) in Providence, Rhode Island, in July 2006. The director was Lowry Marshall; the production stage manager was Robin Grady. The cast was:

SOLOMON	Steven Levenson
DIWATA	Lucy DeVito
HOWIE	Justin Blanchard
TEACHER	Darius Pierce
REPORTER	Crystal Finn

Speech & Debate received its world premiere at the Roundabout Theatre Company (Todd Haimes, Artistic Director; Harold Wolpert, Managing Director; Julia C. Levy, Executive Director) as the inaugural production of Roundabout Underground, at the Harold & Miriam Steinberg Center for Theatre, in New York City, on October 23, 2007. It was directed by Jason Moore; the set design was by Anna Louizos, the costume design was by Heather Dunbar, the lighting design was by Justin Townsend, the sound and projection design was by Brett Jarvis, the choreography was by Boo Killebrew; Howie/Solomon's art was by Lowry Marshall/Steven Levenson, original music was composed by Stephen Karam; the production stage manager was Cyrille Blackburn. The cast was:

SOLOMON	Jason Fuchs
DIWATA	Sarah Steele
HOWIE	Gideon Glick
TEACHER/REPORTER	Susan Blackwell

Speech & Debate was produced in Chicago at American Theater Company (PJ Paparelli, Artistic Director) in April 2008. It was directed by PJ Paparelli; the set design was by Keith Pitts, the costume design was by Myron Elliott, Jr., the lighting design was by Charlie Cooper, the sound design was by Lindsay Jones and Scotty Iseri, the choreography was by Ed Kross, the video/projection design was by Marty Higginbotham and Bobby Richards; original music was composed by Stephen Karam, and the production stage manager was Dana M. Nestrick. The cast was:

SOLOMON	Jared McGuire
DIWATA	Sadieh Rifai
HOWIE	Patrick Andrews
TEACHER/REPORTER	Cheryl Graeff

Speech & Debate received its UK premiere in London by Defibrillator (James Hillier, Artistic Director; Trish Wadley, Executive Producer) at Trafalgar Studios on February 22, 2017. It was directed by Tom Attenborough; the design was by Francesca Reidy; the costume supervisor was Natalie Pryce; the lighting design was by Christopher Nairne, the sound design was by Simon Slater, the video design was by Duncan McLean and Stan Orwin-Fraser; the movement director was Shelby Williams, and the deputy stage manager was Katie Jackson. The cast was:

SOLOMON	Tony Revolori
DIWATA	Patsy Ferran
HOWIE	Douglas Booth
TEACHER/REPORTER	Charlotte Lucas

SCENE BREAKDOWN

Scene 1:   Poetry Reading
Scene 2:   Lincoln-Douglas Debate
Scene 3:   Extemporaneous Commentary
Scene 4:   Storytelling
Scene 5:   Dramatic/Humorous Interpretation
Scene 6:   Cross-Examination Debate
Scene 7:   Duo Interpretation
Scene 8:   Declamation
Scene 9:   Group Interpretation
Scene 10: Oral Interpretation of Prose
Scene 11: Student Congress
Scene 12: Original Oratory

NOTES

Scene titles should be projected at the start of each scene.

Scene 10 was included in the original New York production; it was cut in subsequent productions. The show may be performed without it at the producing theater's discretion.

A slash (/) means the character with the next line of dialogue begins his or her speech.

CHARACTERS

SOLOMON, sixteen
DIWATA, seventeen
HOWIE, eighteen
TEACHER/REPORTER, female, over forty

Note: the Teacher and Reporter should be played by one actress. These roles are not caricatures.

PLACE

Salem, Oregon

Children should not be asked to touch anyone in the areas of their body that would be covered by a bathing suit or allow anyone to touch them in those areas.

—SHERIFF'S OFFICE, MARION COUNTY, OREGON

DANNYBOY	what do you like about youth?
THERIGHTBI-GUY	energy,
THERIGHTBI-GUY	wonder,
DANNYBOY	personally i like the tight ass
DANNYBOY	lol
DANNYBOY	but thats just me
DANNYBOY	lol
THERIGHTBI-GUY	their hopes for the future. and their whole life in front of them
DANNYBOY	so their innocence?
THERIGHTBI-GUY	no, i don't think. i didn't think of you as an innocent
DANNYBOY	thats good . . . cuz i'm not

—FROM A TRANSCRIPT OF AN ONLINE CHAT, DATED 11/30/04, BETWEEN THE FORMER MAYOR OF SPOKANE, WASHINGTON, JIM WEST ("THERIGHTBI-GUY"), AND AN EIGHTEEN-YEAR-OLD MALE ("DANNYBOY").

SCENE 1

POETRY READING

The stage should be relatively spare, dominated by a large screen or back wall onto which various slides/images can be projected.

With a loud tympani crash, there is a total blackout.

Lights up on an eighteen-year-old boy, Howie. He has his computer keyboard on his lap and is in the middle of an instant-message chat.

Howie's screen name is "BlBoi"; the unseen stranger he is communicating with is "BiGuy." Their names appear on the screen in two different colors.

Throughout the following silent scene, an "instant-message" online conversation is projected.

The dialogue's projection is timed precisely with the music from Aaron Copland's Fanfare for the Common Man. *The result is a choreographed musical number. A cyber-ballet.*

```
BIGUY    Im scared
BLBOI    Y?
BIGUY    u r 2 young
BLBOI    says who?
BIGUY    the police
```

Howie searches for clip art on his computer, finds a picture, pastes it, presses return.

```
BLBOI    [image of a crying baby]
BIGUY    LOL
BLBOI    Im 18
BLBOI    Blonde
BLBOI    Smooth
BLBOI    Lean
BLBOI    Legal
BIGUY    You're of age?
BLBOI    in OR
BIGUY    Are you sure?
BLBOI    yessiree
BIGUY    :)
BLBOI    [emoji: dancing woman in red dress]
BIGUY    I like you
BLBOI    U like youth
BLBOI    right?
BIGUY    Yes
BLBOI    Why?
BIGUY    Hmmmmmm . . .
BIGUY    Energy
BIGUY    Wonder
BIGUY    Optimism
BLBOI    Tight ass
BIGUY    LOL
BLBOI    LOL
BIGUY    [laughing GIF]
BIGUY    [emoji: laughing with tears]
```

Howie makes sure no one is outside his door.

```
BIGUY    im 36
```

Howie reacts, disappointed.

BIGUY	That 2 old?
BLBOI	Not 2 old . . .
BIGUY	. . . but . . .
BLBOI	R
BLBOI	U
BLBOI	Generu$?
BIGUY	Send a pic

Howie searches for clip art on his computer, finds a picture, pastes it, presses return.

BLBOI	[image of a baby at a computer keyboard]
BIGUY	not funny.

Howie poses, takes a picture of himself shirtless in time with the music.

Snap, flash.

He takes another picture.

Snap, flash.

He returns to the computer.

BLBOI	Whats yur job?
BIGUY	I cant say
BIGUY	Im discreet
BLBOI	Closet case
BIGUY	:(
BLBOI	Priest?
BIGUY	No
BLBOI	Pope?
BIGUY	Yes
BLBOI	That's hot
BIGUY	Will wear my pointy hat
BIGUY	When u visit the Vatican
BLBOI	LOL

BIGUY	Meet me now
BLBOI	Where?
BIGUY	Riverfront Park
BLBOI	When?
BIGUY	Midnight
BLBOI	K
BIGUY	send your pics
BIGUY	to?
BIGUY	dramedy@gmail.com

Howie is shocked upon seeing the email address. He stands up, nervous. Something has taken him completely by surprise.

The tympani roll at the end of Fanfare for the Common Man *climaxes with a blackout.*

SCENE 2

LINCOLN-DOUGLAS DEBATE

Lights up on Solomon, sixteen. He stands with a few loose-leaf papers in hand. He is speaking with a female teacher. She is gathering her belongings, getting ready to leave.

SOLOMON

Why can't I write about abortion?

TEACHER

This is the principal's decision, Solomon. It's too controversial, parents complain every time without fail—

SOLOMON

But isn't that the point of the school paper, to create a forum for students to discuss issues actually affecting us? Why ban the most controversial issues?

TEACHER

Abortion is the only topic that is off-limits.

SOLOMON

How about religion?

TEACHER

You can't write about religion.

SOLOMON

Why not?

TEACHER

Separation of church and state, you know this. Other than that, the principal has been very clear: no abortion op-eds. No pro-choice pieces, no pro-life pieces. I'm sorry.

SOLOMON

What about an article about the mayor?

TEACHER

That would be fine.

SOLOMON

And how he's had sex with teenagers?

Teacher sighs. Solomon takes out a newspaper.

SOLOMON

It's in today's *Statesman Journal*, have you read it?

TEACHER

I've glanced at the headlines.

SOLOMON

Our fifty-five-year-old mayor has had sex with three teenage boys.

TEACHER

The facts are not known—

SOLOMON

The facts are that he's a right-wing Republican, an opponent of gay rights and is now accused of having secret online relationships with several teenage boys.

TEACHER

These stories take time to unfold, we won't know the truth for some time—

SOLOMON

Which is why my article is more about the pattern I've discovered, a—

TEACHER

A pattern?

SOLOMON

—a pattern of Republican politicians—I've been researching this on the internet—even in the last few years alone—

TEACHER

You sound as if you've already started writing this, you never received my approval—

SOLOMON

(reading from his notes)
In 2004—just let me read this bit—David Dreier, twelve-term Republican congressman who voted for a measure that banned gays from adopting in Washington, DC, is revealed to be, surprise, living with a man—

TEACHER

Solomon, I'm not sure what—

SOLOMON

—2006, Mark Foley is sexting interns in the Capitol building—which, any idiot should know those files will be stored in your cache—

TEACHER
Your what—?

SOLOMON
—and no one's learning any lessons, there's Ed Schrock, Ted Haggard—

TEACHER

Can you wrap it up, please—

—Larry Craig, Bob Allen—he's my favorite, Florida co-chairman of the McCain campaign. The man introduced legislation to outlaw people from quote "intentionally masturbating" in public, and—as opposed to *accidentally* masturbating?—

(back to notes)

—he then gets caught in a bathroom offering a police officer *twenty bucks for a blowjob!*—

TEACHER

Okay—

SOLOMON

—and now it's happening right here in Salem—our mayor has opposed every bit of gay-rights legislation proposed in Oregon and yet—

TEACHER

Slow down, first of all, you're making these issues uniquely Republican, you could easily research similar Democratic scandals, President Clinton—

SOLOMON

—but people expect that kind of behavior from Democrats—

TEACHER

Solomon—

SOLOMON

—I'm just saying, my piece is exploring the phenomenon of *Republican conservatives*, politicians who spend their careers championing morality, American values, *the sanctity of marriage*—people like our mayor, Ted Cruz, Mike Pence who—

TEACHER

Mike Pence is not gay—

SOLOMON

Well, not yet, but the pattern—

TEACHER

You're trying to cause a stir, and I—

SOLOMON

I'm trying to figure out how a man can make the decision to live a fictional life *so fully* that he becomes capable of *publicly* pushing policy that cuts against . . . who he is.

TEACHER

Have you talked to your parents about this?

SOLOMON

No, they think I'm writing about abortion, this topic would be too controversial for them.

Beat.

TEACHER

Right, well . . . the fact that you don't feel comfortable speaking to your parents about your new topic . . . maybe that's what *I'm* feeling . . .

SOLOMON

You need to read this to appreciate how good this is, there's / —hold on . . .

TEACHER

Solomon, please . . .

SOLOMON

The editor of the newspaper confronts our mayor and asks . . .
    (*reading from the paper*)
"Mr. Mayor, why don't you just come clean and tell me that being gay is part of who you are. We have several transcripts from gay.com in which you admit to your fondness for young men."
    (*to Teacher*)
But the amazing thing is, the mayor refuses to come out. Even after being caught, even after all of the evidence, the mayor says:
    (*reading*)
"I am a straight man who likes to mentor kids." On *gay.com*?!

TEACHER

Solomon, *enough.*

SOLOMON
Are you mad because you supported his campaign?

TEACHER
Excuse me?

SOLOMON
I have a program here from a fund-raising dinner listing you as a sponsor for the mayor's county initiative. You're listed under "fifty dollars or less." I googled you.

The Teacher notices Solomon's iPhone.

TEACHER
What are you doing? Have you been recording me?

SOLOMON
Yes. I have a release form here for you to sign. At the end of our talk. If you don't mind.

TEACHER
I'm not signing anything. Why would I sign something? And please turn that off.

SOLOMON
But you did support his campaign?

TEACHER
What? That has absolutely nothing to do with my disapproving your topic. And please *turn that off*.

SOLOMON
Are you a Log Cabin Republican?

TEACHER
Am I—what?

SOLOMON
The *Oregonian* says he's the first Republican mayor in fifteen years to lose the backing of the Salem chapter of that group, / I'm wondering why—

No, of course I'm not. I'm not even—of course I'm not—

SOLOMON

You're not what? What is a Log Cabin Republican?

TEACHER

You know what, why don't you ask your parents.

SOLOMON

I'll google it.

TEACHER

Google it, then. Good.

SOLOMON

I know you're not a lesbian.

TEACHER

Solomon!

SOLOMON

I'm just saying, why would I have to ask my parents? Why can't we talk about anything real in school? Why is everybody so nervous?

TEACHER

Stop recording me.

SOLOMON

I'm sorry.

He turns it off.

SOLOMON

I'm thinking of writing a separate, bigger piece about freedom of speech in high schools. If it's good I can have my dad pitch it to his friend who works at the *Oregonian*. My dad's a lawyer, he knows tons of people.

TEACHER

Is this why you keep choosing controversial subjects? So I can reject them and fuel your story?

SOLOMON

No.

TEACHER

Because your father was one of the parents who complained to the principal about some of the topics the paper has published this year. I thought you were aware of this.

Beat.

SOLOMON

No. He didn't—no, I didn't know . . . I can't believe he talked to you . . .

TEACHER

Talk to your parents about this. Please.

SOLOMON

Everyone always says that: "Talk to your parents," "Ask your parents"—why can't we talk about these things in school?

TEACHER

The school district has several forums—there are at least three assemblies every year—

SOLOMON

Yes, I know—have you ever sat in on one of them? There's the stranger-danger session where we are told by some experts not to let anyone touch us in our bathing-suit areas. That's what they say. Our *bathing-suit areas*. Half of our class is having real-life sex and—I'm not, but—and they're talking to us about our bathing-suit areas? Our *bathing-suit areas*? Why don't they talk about stuff we actually want to know about, like how do you actually *do* oral sex and—

TEACHER

Okay, time's up, / I'm sorry—

SOLOMON

I'm going to write this story.

Beat.

TEACHER

Have you considered finding another outlet for all of this energy? What about Speech and Debate? The school's looking to start up the first team.

SOLOMON

No, I don't like public speaking, you're trying to change the subject—

TEACHER

Miss Langan is looking for a student volunteer to learn about the different events; someone to raise student interest now so that the club can hit the ground running next year.

SOLOMON

Every morning when it's announced people laugh, everyone thinks it's a joke.

TEACHER

Why don't you learn about the different events—

SOLOMON

I'll google it . . .

TEACHER

Google it, then, good.

Solomon starts to put his iPhone away.

SOLOMON

So do you have any other comments? Clarifications before we end the interview?

TEACHER

It's not an interview, and if you use any of my quotes out of context, I'll personally escort you to the principal's office.

Beat.

SOLOMON

(iPhone still in hand)
I could write an article about how Abraham Lincoln was a homosexual.

TEACHER

Solomon!

SOLOMON

In Civics class, you told us—

TEACHER

No, I did not! You asked me if—I mentioned in passing that several historians—I never, I *stressed* that there is no evidence to—Solomon, are you recording me? . . .

SOLOMON

Was I supposed to turn it off?

TEACHER

Yes!

SOLOMON	TEACHER
Sorry, sorry . . .	Just, okay, just let me speak to the principal, okay? Let's see what Miss Langan says and I'll get back to you. Okay?

Beat. Solomon smiles.

SOLOMON

Thank you.

Blackout.

SCENE 3

EXTEMPORANEOUS COMMENTARY

Diwata's bedroom. A Casio keyboard and four empty wine coolers are on the floor.

She pushes the "playback" button on her keyboard.

A few chords sound, playing over and over. She checks her computer, picks up the microphone attached to it and begins to sing.

Her opening verse is more mellow and melancholy than loud and showy. Also, her one-word blurts at the end of her singing sections (i.e., "nice," "solid," "fierce," etc.) are sincere (and kind of weird) compliments to herself.

DIWATA
Sittin' at my Casio keyboard
Thank God it's built to pre-record
Otherwise I couldn't play and sing
At the same time

I'm . . .

Sittin' at my Casio keyboard
Kinda drunk and
Really fuckin' bored
Otherwise I'd have better things to do
Than update my blog

On a Friday night.

Diwata has some more to drink.

Welcome to the first podcast entry of my diary, updated daily at monoblog.com. Let's hear it for my band—that's Casio in the background. Casio's been programmed to play the only three chords I know over and over while I improvise a new song, live, before your ears, America. Ideally, the music would be a little more interesting, but I can't play and sing at the same time, and I have no friends to help me out. "But Diwata," you're saying to yourselves, "you're so odd and frumpy—you must have friends." But no, I don't. All I have is my music.

Singing, improvising:

There is music in my body.

She turns her keyboard off.

Nice. The upcoming auditions for this year's spring musical were the inspiration for this live, streaming musical entry. My high school will be doing the timeless classic *Once Upon a Mattress*, and this year, like every other year, I will not get cast because of my talentless drama teacher—a man I'll call gay-guy-with-a-receding-hairline in order to protect Mr. Walter M. Healy's anonymity. But this year, I think *America* should decide whether or not I get to showcase my skills in North Salem High's multipurpose room. "But Diwata," you're asking, "how can we show you our undying love?" Calm yourselves, I'll tell you. You see, Mr. Healy was foolish enough to include his email address on the bottom of his class syllabus; so I say, let the e-campaign begin: if you think that I should play the lead in the spring play, write to the fool at dramedy@gmail.com. That's D-R-A-M-E-D-Y at gmail.com.

She turns the keyboard on, starting the musical vamp.

Mr. Healy, this verse . . . is for you.

Singing:

> Mr. Healy you're a crap sandwich
> I'm pure and you're a crap sandwich
> Get some bread, your balding head, and some more bread
> You have your head between bread
> Crap sandwich . . . yeah . . .

Pleased with her work:

Fierce. I totally improv'd that. That's right—what you heard was free-form, free-flow, yo ho, yo ho, but I know some people listening are gonna go, "Maybe it's Ms. Monoblog who's the freak," they're saying. Well, I happen to know firsthand that it's Mr. Healy who's got problems . . . let's just say our fine mayor isn't the only one keeping secrets . . . but if you still think Ms. Monoblog is just a crazy drama queen, allow me to share a brief story with you that will clear all this up.

Diwata stops the musical vamp.

At Friday's drama club meeting, Mr. Healy proudly announced that he will be altering the plot of our spring musical, *Once Upon a Mattress*, ever so slightly, to make it more appropriate for the needs of our conservative community. Lady Larken, the character who needs to get married ASAP because she is pregnant out of wedlock, will no longer be pregnant. That's right—to avoid the raciness of an unwed mom, Lady Larken will just really, *really* want to get married. We have a *teen mothers program* at our high school, and the man thinks an unwed mother is too racy for us?

Diwata starts the musical vamp again, rallying the troops.

Are we in Salem, Oregon or Salem, Massachusetts, circa sixteen-twenty-whenever-those-witches-were-bein'-hunted.

Singing:

> Well you can't burn me
> This witch is fireproof
> So try and hang me
> And see how strong my neck is.

Bold. That's an excerpt from "Headstrong," a ballad from my new original musical *Crucible*, based on Arthur Miller's play, *THE Crucible*. The show is told entirely from the perspective of Mary Warren, a part I was born to play, and a part I was denied last year by the man who shall remain nameless, Mr. Walter M. Healy. Currently, *Crucible* is on hiatus until I rewrite the plot or until Arthur fucking Miller's estate agrees to release the rights to me. Whatever.

Singing:

> Try to burn me
> But you'll be dead wrong
> You can try to hang me
> But this girl is headstrong.

She turns the music off.

Wicked. Enough about me. Right now, I'm worried about the composer of *Once Upon a Mattress*, Mary Rodgers. Because once she hears about Mr. Healy's heinous changes, she will die. And if she's already dead, she will karate-kick her way out of her coffin to find Mr. Healy and slap him in the balls.

She pushes play on her Casio and starts the musical vamp. The music plays under the following:

And so, an impromptu dirge for Miss Mary . . .

Singing:

> Oh . . . oh . . .

Lights come up on Howie and Solomon in front of their computers in their bedrooms. They are listening to Diwata's podcast. Howie has headphones on and is finding it thoroughly entertaining. He bops his head along with the beat.

All the guys sing . . .

Howie sings along with the broadcast, singing the same "dirge for Mary Rodgers" with Diwata.

DIWATA AND HOWIE

Oh . . . oh . . .

DIWATA

And all the ladies go . . .

Solomon now joins in with Diwata, while Howie sticks with his original vocal line.

DIWATA AND SOLOMON

Oh-ee . . . oh-ee . . . oh-ee . . . oh-ee . . . oh-ee . . . oh-ee . . . oh . . . woa . . . oh . . .

HOWIE
(simultaneously with the above)

Oh . . . oh . . .

All three now sing their own parts together.

HOWIE

Oh . . . oh . . .

SOLOMON
(simultaneously with the above)

Oh-ee . . . oh-ee . . . oh-ee . . . oh-ee . . . oh-ee . . . oh-ee . . . oh . . . woa . . . oh . . .

DIWATA
(simultaneously with Howie and Solomon)

Sittin' at my Casio keyboard
Thank God it's built to pre-record
Otherwise I couldn't play and sing
At the same time

I'm—

The following three voices all overlap:

VOICE (DIWATA'S MOTHER)
(overlapping)
Diwata, that is the most annoying thing I've ever heard in my life.

VOICE (SOLOMON'S FATHER)
(overlapping)
Solomon, what are you doing? Are you *singing?*

VOICE (HOWIE'S MOTHER)
(overlapping)
I'm trying to sleep, Howie, please . . .

Beat. All three are embarrassed.

DIWATA
We're having technical difficulties, so I leave you with this: Lady Larken and I have a lot in common. We aren't both perfectly pretty, and I don't have Lady Larken's perfect soprano voice. But we had something in common until you messed everything up.
(she feels her stomach)
Fuck you, Mr. Healy.

Lights shift. Focus on Howie, who is busy typing. His message is projected on the screen. It reads:

"liked your blog entry. Got my own dirt on Healy. yur right—mayor isn't the only one keeping secrets. Hit me up."
                    —message posted by BlBoi@icloud.com at 10:58PM

Blackout.

SCENE 4

STORYTELLING

In the blackout we hear a phone ring. Howie picks up the call, we hear his voice in the dark:

HOWIE

Hello?

Lights up on Solomon, also on the phone.

SOLOMON

Hi, I'm looking for the person who owns the screen-name "B-L Boy"? It's linked to a Mac account—"Boy" is spelled "B-O-I."

HOWIE

Who is this?

SOLOMON

I'm a reporter, from the *Trojan*. I just read a post on a website called "monoblog.com"—your email helped me find your Facebook profile which listed this phone number. The post read:

"Got my own dirt on Healy. yur right—mayor isn't the only one keeping secrets."

> HOWIE
I posted that for the girl who did the podcast—

> SOLOMON
I'm working on a story for the *Trojan* involving the mayor's sex scandal. I'd like to interview you.

> HOWIE
Why do you want to interview *me*?

> SOLOMON
Your message implies that Mr. Healy has also had relationships with younger guys, like the mayor. That might be newsworthy. He *is* a high school / teacher.

> HOWIE
Wait, is the *Trojan*—is that the *school* / paper?

> SOLOMON
Don't hang up, please. I just want to find out what you know about Mr. Healy.

> HOWIE
No, sorry—

> SOLOMON
I know you think I'm not a real reporter, but I have lots of experience, I've already won some awards.

> HOWIE
Like what kind of experience? What kind of awards?

> SOLOMON
Like, if you want specific details, like, honorable mention in the National Write and Illustrate Your Own Book Contest / and I'm—

HOWIE

I got third place in that contest when I was in fifth grade. Isn't it only open to younger / kids only? . . .

SOLOMON

I'm also—let me finish . . . I'm the first sophomore to become an associate editor of / the *Trojan*—

HOWIE

. . . and isn't it called the *Oregon* Write and Illustrate Your Own Book Contest? It's not national. Why should I talk to you?—

SOLOMON

Because you posted a private message to a public website, and I read it. And I can direct anyone to that website, including Mr. Healy or real reporters who will cover the story and find out your secret whether you want them to or not.

HOWIE

(angrily)
Dude, relax, okay? Don't do that, don't be a freak. *Please* . . .

SOLOMON

I won't, I'm sorry.

Beat.

HOWIE

So . . . good-bye. Okay?

Beat.

SOLOMON

What was your story about?

HOWIE

What?

SOLOMON

You said you got third place, so I'm just asking—

What? Why the hell / would you ask—

SOLOMON
You don't have to tell me if—

HOWIE
I'm not going to tell you. Good-bye, okay?

SOLOMON
Tell me or I'll call Mr. Healy.

Howie is pissed off. He holds the phone away from him. He's unsure what to do.

SOLOMON
What was it about?
   (beat)
Are you there?

Beat.

HOWIE
   (holding back his anger)
It was about this kid who travels back in time.

SOLOMON
How far back?

HOWIE
Very far back, to like, biblical times, okay?

SOLOMON
Like in a time machine? How does he do that?

HOWIE
I don't remember. Good-bye, okay?

SOLOMON
Who does he meet? / What does he do?

HOWIE

Jesus Christ . . . he meets some other guy, Cain.

SOLOMON

Like, Cain from the Bible?

HOWIE

You don't know when you read it, but it's biblical times, so you figure it out.

SOLOMON

What happens to Cain?

HOWIE

Why do you care?

SOLOMON

Tell me.

HOWIE

Or what?

SOLOMON

Or . . . I might . . . call Mr. Healy.

Beat. Howie is angry. He collects himself, proceeds . . .

HOWIE

Cain is like, totally put off by how queeny the time-travel kid is.

SOLOMON

The time-travel kid is queeny? How would people know that?

HOWIE

My illustrations . . .

Projection of one of Howie's illustrations: a picture of a mascu-line Cain, perhaps with a club, disapproving of a modern queeny kid. It is well drawn for a ten year old.

SOLOMON

Okay, okay—so then what? What does the queeny kid do?

HOWIE

I told you, he time-travels.

SOLOMON

And he meets Cain?

HOWIE

Yes.

SOLOMON

And . . . they do—what do they do?

HOWIE

Nothing. Cain hates him. So he goes to kill him.

SOLOMON

The queeny kid? Why would Cain kill the queeny kid?

HOWIE

Because he's pissed off that this kid is all gay and queeny, and Cain wants him dead.

SOLOMON

Okay, okay, that's abrupt, but okay . . .

HOWIE

And right before Cain strikes him down, the kid whispers in his ear . . .

Projection: illustration of the queeny kid whispering in Cain's ear.

HOWIE

"Your brother is just like me."

SOLOMON

What does that mean?

(*obviously*)
It means Cain's brother is gay . . .

SOLOMON
Abel? Abel is gay? How would the queeny kid know that?

HOWIE
Gaydar, I don't remember. I was nine.

SOLOMON
Okay, okay . . . and then . . . and then, what?

HOWIE
Cain kills the kid.

Projection: Cain standing over a bloody queeny kid.

HOWIE
And then Cain kills his brother. The end.

Projection: Cain standing over two *bloody queeny kids.*

SOLOMON
So this is confusing. You changed the Bible story? So that Cain really killed Abel because Abel was gay?

HOWIE
Yes.

SOLOMON
That is so confusing . . . and you got third place? . . .

Howie smiles in disbelief at Solomon's seriousness.

HOWIE
It's pretty messed up because I wrote it when I was nine, right after I came out.

SOLOMON
You came out when you were nine?

HOWIE

Yeah—well, ten officially.

SOLOMON

So why isn't your time-travel kid in the Bible? How do you explain that?

HOWIE

Are you really this serious?

SOLOMON

What?

HOWIE

Never mind. Are we done?

SOLOMON

I'm not serious.

HOWIE

Okay . . .

SOLOMON

Why would you say that? —You act like— / what is that . . . ?

HOWIE

Wow, you're a freak.

SOLOMON

I'm not a freak. I'm just not serious in some bad way.

HOWIE

Really?

SOLOMON

Yeah . . .

HOWIE

Good for you.

Yeah, good for me.

I bet your *story* was serious.

SOLOMON

Not in a bad way, no. Actually, it was historical fiction–slash–action adventure, actually.

HOWIE

Oh yeah?

SOLOMON

Yeah.

HOWIE

Good. So have I answered all your / questions?—

SOLOMON

It was about Abraham Lincoln—

HOWIE

No, I don't need to know / this—

SOLOMON

No, I know—but he's a teenager in my story, though, like fourteen, I'm just saying, which was kind of creative to write about Abraham Lincoln as a boy since most people think of him as a man that's all I'm saying. So—

HOWIE

Did he have like acne, how did you draw him young?

SOLOMON

No, I studied historical portraits from the period.

Projection: Solomon's illustration of a very poorly drawn (border-line stick figure) teenage Abraham Lincoln.

SOLOMON

And it's basically about teenage Abraham Lincoln meeting this girl in the library in his town, and the girl hates to read and learn . . . and over the course of this rainy day, he teaches her to love reading and love learning.

Projection: an illustration of poorly drawn teenage Abraham Lincoln with poorly drawn girl in town. The girl looks very boyish, wearing overalls. They hold hands.

SOLOMON

Because he really did love those things in real life, it was based on, on his real . . . oh my God, my story sounds terrible . . .

HOWIE

Yeah.

SOLOMON

It's bad, isn't it? I mean I was only eleven, but—

HOWIE

I wouldn't worry about it.

SOLOMON

No, I'm not worried about it. I'm not *worried* about it.

HOWIE

Good.

SOLOMON

Very good.
    (*beat*)
So, good-bye, I guess.

HOWIE

Yeah—and you're not going to call Mr.—

SOLOMON

I won't do that, no.

Thank you—

SOLOMON

Have you won other awards besides that third place?—

HOWIE

What? / Oh my God . . .

SOLOMON

It's a simple question.

HOWIE

Why do you care? / You're such a freak—

SOLOMON

You *haven't* won any other awards . . .

HOWIE

Uh, let me see . . . I was an Eagle Scout at fifteen. That was good. I haven't cured cancer or anything.

SOLOMON

I thought you couldn't be a Boy Scout if you were, you know—

HOWIE

No—well, I mean this one time I even made up a dance for a Scout talent show, like an actual dance I choreographed to George Michael's "Freedom." So, maybe they didn't know, but I mean . . . *that* was gay.

SOLOMON

What kind of dance?

HOWIE

(losing patience)
It wasn't a *kind* of dance, I just had all these special moves I made up, that I was going to teach to everybody—

SOLOMON

What made them special? What were your moves?

HOWIE

They weren't really special, I made them up in my bedroom so, you know, they were my moves, that's all I mean.

SOLOMON

Okay, I'm with you, and then . . .

HOWIE

Then what?

SOLOMON

Did they like your moves, what?

HOWIE

That's not the point.

SOLOMON

They *didn't* like your moves—?

HOWIE

I didn't do them, why do you ask so many questions, you're / such a freak . . .

SOLOMON

Why didn't you do them?

HOWIE

Because I got there and the other guys were doing all this shit, tying knots, throwing curveballs . . . the kid before me did some lame wrestling moves, how to pin someone or something—*of course I didn't do them*, I'm not an idiot.

SOLOMON

You just, didn't do them?—

HOWIE

Dude, yes, of course, yes!

Beat.

SOLOMON

People in Salem are pretty open-minded.

HOWIE

People in Salem are straight. I don't know, I'm new here, I grew up in Portland, but . . . people here think they're liberal, but most are like liberal puritans. I can't even find a teacher to be the advisor for the gay-straight alliance.

SOLOMON

Is that like— / what is—?

HOWIE

It's not a big deal, I just need to find an advisor or else I don't get any school funding.

SOLOMON

Well . . . have you asked the mayor? I bet he'd do it . . .

HOWIE

Right, our mayor who won't give me any civil rights, but *will* give me a blowjob . . .

SOLOMON

That's disgusting . . .

HOWIE

You're disgusting, stop freaking out about stuff so much, you're like an old man—

SOLOMON

I'm not an old man, I'm not—why would you . . . I'm not an old man . . . and . . .

(*beat*)

I'm not an old man. But, I don't know, sometimes I think the best part of being young is knowing that there are all of these unhappy older people around who wish they were my age.

(*beat*)

Like, the good part isn't going to football games or house parties . . . it's just . . . the best part is being envied. Is that awful?

HOWIE

You're very serious . . .

SOLOMON

You're very serious . . .

Beat.

HOWIE

You want to know the truth about Mr. Healy?

SOLOMON

Yes. *Yes.*

Solomon pushes a button on his phone.

HOWIE

I haven't told anyone this . . .

Blackout.

SCENE 5

Dramatic/Humorous Interpretation

A sign that reads: SPEECH AND DEBATE—BE THE 1ST TEAM MEMBERS OF NORTH SALEM'S NEWEST CLUB!

Diwata and Solomon are the only people in the room. Diwata stands in front. Solomon sits, observing. She lifts her head to signal the beginning of her introduction.

DIWATA
(speaking to an imaginary audience)
In Salem, everything and everyone belongs to either God or the Devil; dissent is not merely unlawful, it is associated with satanic activity. As Danforth says in Act III, "a person is either with this court or he must be counted against it." And so, in the following scene from Arthur Miller's classic, *The Crucible*, I invite you to enter a world in which some girls are good and some girls are bitches who pretend to be witches, hot flow, yo ho, and so, get ready to know a girl named Mary Warren. Accused of witchcraft, Mary stands before the court unsure of whether or not telling the truth will set her free, or set her on fire.

Solomon looks around to see if anyone else has entered. Or understands what Diwata is saying. Diwata checks an index card.

DIWATA

The townsfolk became active in all of the madness not merely out of religious piety and Goody goodness; but also because it allowed them to act out every dark desire and hateful urge under the cover of righteousness. The secrets the girls released were able to thrive only because other people benefited from them. What good is a secret, if people can keep it?
   (beat)
With that in mind, get ready, because something wicked this way is coming, and if you feel flames, don't pull the fire alarm . . . it's just feeling hot because things are really heating up . . . in . . . *The Crucible*, by Arthur Miller.

Diwata drops her head, preparing for her performance.

With each of the following lines of dialogue, Diwata changes her focal point (and possibly her voice) to indicate that she is becoming "another character." Her attempt is earnest, not psychotic.

DIWATA

   (as Danforth)
You are charging Abigail Williams with a marvelous cool plot to murder, do you understand that?
   (as Proctor)
I do, sir. I believe she means to murder.
   (as Danforth)
This child would murder your wife?
   (as Proctor)
It is not a child, sir. It is a whore.

Solomon raises his hand, interrupts.

SOLOMON

I'm sorry, I have no idea what you're doing. What are you doing?

DIWATA

Please don't interrupt. Just experience my demonstration first, then I'll explain the rules, 'kay?

Diwata drops her head in preparation for her performance. She raises her head and begins again.

DIWATA

(*as Danforth*)
You are charging Abigail Williams with a marvelous cool plot to murder, do you understand that?
(*as Proctor*)
I do, sir. I believe she means to murder.
(*as Danforth*)
This child would murder your wife?
(*as Proctor*)
It is not a child, sir. It is a whore.

Solomon raises his hand, interrupts.

SOLOMON

Okay, I'm not even following—

DIWATA

This category is called "Dramatic Interpretation" and I'm performing a scene from *The Crucible*. You perform all of the parts of the play yourself, that's what you do for this event.

SOLOMON

Why would you do that, perform all of the parts?

DIWATA

Because those are the rules of the National Forensics League. People in the know call this category "DI," which is the slang terminology for "Dramatic Interpretation."

SOLOMON

I don't know what you're saying.

DIWATA

Speech and Debate has its own lingo. I'll teach you all the terms, don't worry.

SOLOMON

I'm not / worried . . .

DIWATA

Have you even read *The Crucible*? We did it in the fall, amazing play. I love big fat epic stuff. *Hamlet, Angels in America, Wicked—*

SOLOMON

You were in *The Crucible* here? I saw that. Who did you play?

DIWATA

I was an extra, I looked like a fat pilgrim, whatever. I didn't even have a name. I called myself Goody Goodyear.

SOLOMON

That's funny.

DIWATA

I didn't even get cast as Tituba. Healy said she was black, which—historically the character was Native Indian, or South American Arawak, some shit like that—so . . . whatever, I can't believe I didn't get Tituba. Whatever.

SOLOMON

That sucks.

DIWATA

Yeah, but I went as Mary Warren for Halloween which was pretty sweet revenge. I dyed my waitress uniform black and—it looked fierce. I like, *was* Mary Warren. I ran around screaming, having breakdowns—it was amazing. What did you go as last year?

SOLOMON

I didn't go as anything. But wait—which one is Mary Warren?

DIWATA

She's the girl who basically knows that all the other girls are just pretending to be witches, but in the end, she realizes she'll hang if she doesn't lie . . . so she saves herself. She holds it in.

SOLOMON

She lies.

SOLOMON

"Blonde Boy" is a new student here, a transfer. Keep reading . . .

DIWATA

Where did this come from?

SOLOMON

On your website—this kid—"Blonde Boy" posted a message for you—
   (takes out a sheet of paper)
—I printed it out . . .

DIWATA

I know, I saw it, but I don't respond to every freak who posts a comment—

SOLOMON

I did, I called him.

DIWATA

You *called* him?

SOLOMON

I'm a reporter—I wanted to find out the dirt he had on Mr. Healy . . .

DIWATA

And this kid talked to you?

SOLOMON

Yeah, he said they were gonna meet up at Riverfront Park, but then he recognized Healy's email address from his class syllabus and got freaked out . . .

DIWATA

Riverfront Park? Oh my God I'm never going there again . . .

SOLOMON

. . . so I was like, I said to him, "How do I know you're not making all this up," or whatever—and I got him to email me the transcript!

DIWATA

(looking at the transcript)
So this is actually real?

SOLOMON

I'm a reporter, you need to get proof.

DIWATA

If this gets out . . .

SOLOMON

I know, I know . . .

DIWATA

. . . will he be . . . arrested, do you think, or . . .

SOLOMON

Well, he told Healy he wasn't a student—and Blonde Boy's profile still says he's from Portland, so . . .

DIWATA

I can't believe / this . . .

SOLOMON

. . . and, and the kid is eighteen, it wasn't really illegal, but if . . . if *you* know something too . . . it could help define this as a pattern as opposed to—

DIWATA

Sorry, can't help you . . . I just heard some rumors going around about Healy, nothing concrete.

SOLOMON

Well what were the rumors? They might be relevant.

DIWATA

No, I started them.

SOLOMON

Oh. So—

DIWATA

Look, I've answered your questions, and I—I need to focus on Speech and Debate right now, there's a chance I might have latecomers—

SOLOMON

Why are you pretending to care about Speech and Debate— you're only doing it because you can't get a part in the school musical—

DIWATA

I got a part, you asshole! I could have done the show if I wanted.

SOLOMON

You got a part?

DIWATA

Featured ensemble. Which is—for starters, FYI, most kids just got plain old ensemble, number one . . .

SOLOMON

Then why aren't you doing it?

DIWATA

. . . because number two—let me finish—featured ensemble is unacceptable when you spend three weeks preparing your audition song. Any other director would have given me the lead. If you saw my audition you would get it.

SOLOMON

I doubt that.

DIWATA

Screw you! You use cover-up to hide your acne and think people can't tell.

Solomon gets his bookbag, goes to leave.

DIWATA

Do you even *know* what I did for my audition, for *Once Upon a Mattress*?

Huh? . . . no—

DIWATA

The lead in *Once Upon a Mattress*, Winnifred, she sings this big song in Act II that's kind of a mock-striptease number. So I sang the song . . . and underneath all my clothes, I had on a nude bodystocking, so . . . do you see where I'm going with this?

SOLOMON

No.

DIWATA

Well, there I am, belting my brains out and as the song progresses, I start removing bits of my clothing so by the time I finish, all my clothes are on the floor. And I'm wearing nothing but the bodystocking—

SOLOMON

Did it look like you were really nude?

DIWATA

No—I mean, I had no nipples or anything. Nudity wasn't the point.

SOLOMON

Why wouldn't Winnifred have nipples?

DIWATA

That's not the point. I shouldn't have told you. *God.*

SOLOMON

What was the point?

DIWATA

To take a risk, to get noticed. I'm not going to get cast for my golden hair, or tall frame, or cheekbones, I'm, I'm—I actually have pretty good cheekbones, but it's—I'm ready to be noticed. You can't understand, you're not in my profession.

SOLOMON

Well—no, but . . . no, there was this kid who published a novel
when he was twelve, which . . .

Beat.

SOLOMON

But then, some writers don't hit it big until they're older, in
their thirties or forties even.

DIWATA

Yeah, well you'll never hit it big if you keep pursuing stories you
can't get printed . . .

SOLOMON

What does that mean?

DIWATA

Where are you going to publish the piece you're writing? I mean,
the school paper won't let you write about a teacher in the
building . . .

SOLOMON

I know, my dad has this friend at the *Oregonian*, I'm thinking
I can show it to her, they'd publish it there.

DIWATA

But . . . I mean, you realize once you show it to her, she'll pass it
off to a *real* journalist to write the *actual* story. I mean . . . right?

SOLOMON

But—and I *am* a real journalist, / first of all . . .

DIWATA

You are a kid who obviously has some weird agenda—

SOLOMON

Shuttup, I don't have—I'm, obviously, yes, I want to get my foot
in the door as a writer, but it's—

You're not going to get your foot in the door that way, trust me . . . but . . .

SOLOMON

What?

DIWATA

(subtly proceeding with her plan)
. . . no, I'm just thinking, I could help you out if you wanted . . . I could, if you wanted, I could make your article part of my Speech and Debate presentation. I could have your words read in front of the entire school board if you helped me by joining / the team—

SOLOMON

No thank you—I don't like performing . . .

DIWATA

There are lots of categories—we could use "Original Oratory," I could read your article word for word as a speech, think of it as broadcast journalism—

SOLOMON

No, okay?

DIWATA

Can you imagine having all of these school-board members behind a long table listening to us . . . wondering, "Who is this fierce talent? Why the hell wasn't *she* Laurey in last year's production of *Oklahoma*? That other girl they cast didn't even use vibrato / and—"

SOLOMON

What are you / talking about?—

DIWATA

. . . and saying, "*This* boy's writing is undeniably good. Where has *this* kid been hiding, why haven't *his* stories been running on the front of every issue of the *Trojan*?"—

SOLOMON

Well, because the school board thinks—it's *censorship*, three
times they've—I wrote this amazing piece about . . . ugh . . .
yeah, I mean, yes, I do like the idea of . . . I mean, this is a district that won't let me write about abortion or our own mayor's
scandal in the school paper—so yeah, the thought of a forum
in which they are *forced* to listen . . .

DIWATA

Exactly, so just, just consider it . . .

SOLOMON

Wouldn't we . . . get in trouble?

DIWATA

For turning in a child molester? I mean, that's what you think
he is, right? Based on your talk with this kid?

Beat.

SOLOMON

Lemme think about it.

DIWATA

Think about it, yeah . . . I'm just . . . I'm glad you came today.
We do need to find one more person to get funding and some
rehearsal space, you know, but . . . I can do that unless you have
a friend who wants—

SOLOMON

Most of my friends are at other schools or from youth group,
you know?

DIWATA

Oh sure, sure. Mine are mostly older, they've graduated, so . . .

SOLOMON
(*getting out his bookbag*)
Here, let me give you my number . . .

Solomon has to remove his phone to reach a business card in the bottom of his bag. Diwata picks it up, looks at the screen.

DIWATA

You're listening to George Michael? On repeat?

SOLOMON

Oh, yeah, that's—nothing, just wanted to hear a song . . .

Solomon takes his phone back.

DIWATA

You know George Michael was arrested for masturbating in a public bathroom, something like that, right?

SOLOMON

What?

DIWATA

Is that why you like him?

SOLOMON

No. That's disgusting. Why would you say that?

DIWATA

Because I think that's how people remember him.

SOLOMON

I don't know, I think it's disgusting. I'll see you later, my dad's probably waiting for me.

Solomon exits. Diwata spies the piece of paper Solomon left behind, the printout of Howie's post.

She picks it up, thinks.

Blackout.

SCENE 6

CROSS-EXAMINATION DEBATE

Howie sits at a table in a restaurant. Diwata stands next to him, wearing her waitress uniform, coffee pot in hand. The uniform is unflattering—a one-piece "dress" (which goes down to her calves) complete with a white apron in front. Howie is uneasy.

DIWATA

. . . Sometimes, when all the stalls are taken in the girls' room at school, I use the boys' bathroom on the third floor, because no one is ever up there after three. And I shout first, I say, "Anyone in there?" You know, something like that . . .

HOWIE

Can't you sit down? I feel really weird sitting here by myself . . .

DIWATA

I can't take a break for another ten minutes . . . and I have an appointment this afternoon—

HOWIE

Just keep going . . .

                              DIWATA

So last year when we were rehearsing for *The Crucible*, there
was a line of girls, we were all in costume waiting to use the
bathroom . . . so I went up to the third floor, and I yelled into
the boys' room. No one answered, so I went in. I finished going
to the bathroom, and I heard footsteps. Normally, I'd rattle
around, make noise pulling toilet paper out, you know, trying to
let someone know I'm there, I'm a master at masking the sound
of plopping poop.

Howie is not amused.

                              DIWATA

But because this is the guys' bathroom . . . I just kind of hold
my breath, thinking I'll wait it out.

Beat.

                              DIWATA

And then more footsteps. Maybe they came in together, I can't
remember . . . but I could see them through the crack in the
side of the door. Mr. Healy for sure, and then him, with those
white sneakers. Their backs were to me.

                              HOWIE

And you're sure it was him?

                              DIWATA

Positive. He never looked at Mr. Healy, both of them seemed
to be peeing, but then Solomon seemed to be standing further
away from the urinal, like he was . . . I dunno . . . like he was
trying to show Mr. Healy his . . . you know?

Beat.

                              DIWATA

And there was some touching, I don't remember exactly how
it started, because then I breathed, I inhaled, they must have
heard; they didn't check to see who was in the stall, they just
bolted, both of them. And that was it. I sat in there for about
twenty minutes. I was scared. *I* was scared, isn't that weird?

Beat.

DIWATA

Anyway, I brought the Speech and Debate rule book . . .

She puts the Speech and Debate rule book on the table.

DIWATA

I know you only agreed to do one category, but you should consider double-entering. That's the lingo kids use when they do two events, double-entering.

HOWIE

Is it because he's religious? All that Catholic guilty stuff, is that what it is?—

DIWATA

Hey I'm Catholic, that's not it.

HOWIE

You're not practicing, are you?

DIWATA

Just relax, okay? And you should really order something . . .

HOWIE

No. Solomon's getting jerked-off by a teacher after school and he wants to go public with what he knows about *me*? Is he insane? Little closeted faggot . . .

DIWATA

He can't say anything about you. If he wants to talk about you, we talk about him. I'm doing you a favor. I didn't have to tell you any of this. I told you because—

HOWIE

I'm not joining the Speech and Debate team—

DIWATA

You promised—

HOWIE

Please *sit down*. We don't even know each other, this is so weird—

DIWATA

You *promised*, and FYI, it's not weird for me to spend time talking at tables, most customers love me, just FYI—

HOWIE

Why didn't you say something?

DIWATA

When?

HOWIE

Last year, when you saw all that?

DIWATA

What would I have said?—Mom, today I saw a teacher and a student touching each other in their bathing-suit areas?

HOWIE

Bathing— / what?

DIWATA

It's from stranger-danger, you don't remember that? . . .

HOWIE

No, I was in a different / school . . .

DIWATA

I mean, I guess it's better than someone telling me "strangers shouldn't touch your *vagina*," but still—

HOWIE

Okay, be quiet, people are staring.

DIWATA

Obviously you don't want this to get out . . .

HOWIE

If Solomon opens his mouth and I'm known as the pervert cruising for online sex, you think I'm going to get a gay-straight alliance started?

DIWATA

People have their own secrets.

HOWIE

People care. That's why being in Salem is so . . .

Beat.

HOWIE

I hate that straight fraternity dudes can have their porn and Howard Stern can talk about doing women up the ass . . . and they're just normal straight guys—but if there was a *gay* Howard Stern on the air—

DIWATA

I like Howard Stern.

HOWIE

That's not what I'm saying . . .

DIWATA

What does this have to do with Solomon? You're out, you're proud, you can do whatever you want. Probably more things than other minorities. More than women. Stop whining.

HOWIE

No way, no way . . .

DIWATA

Oh, yes, *yes* . . . homophobia is so 1985. Most people think it's cool.

HOWIE

It's not "cool" . . . it's not *trendy* . . . it's *biology* . . .

Shhh . . . I'm just saying—
    (*noticing her manager*)
—spill your coffee or something, help me look busy . . .

HOWIE

What?

DIWATA

Do it!

Howie knocks over his coffee. Diwata pulls out a rag from her apron, sits down and begins to wipe up the table.

HOWIE

Jesus Christ . . .

DIWATA

People our age *don't even have these hang-ups*, by the time we're adults *these won't even be* issues . . .
    (*finishing cleaning up*)
. . . and I didn't mean for you to spill the whole cup. Damnit . . .

Beat.

HOWIE

Would people really think awful things about me if they saw that chat transcript?

DIWATA

I'm a double minority . . .

HOWIE

What, you're—what are you talking about?

DIWATA

If you want to whine about being gay, I'm / just saying . . .

HOWIE

I wasn't whining . . .

DIWATA

. . . I'm female and Filipino.

HOWIE

You don't look Filipino.

DIWATA

You don't look gay.
  (*she smiles*)
Yes you do.

HOWIE

It's the hair, right? Is it the hair?

DIWATA

Yes, Blonde Boy. And PS—what shade of blonde are you—*ebony*?

HOWIE

Shuttup, the name gets guys' attention—and, I bleached my
hair last summer, so—

DIWATA

My grandmother was half Filipino. I'm an eighth. My kids some
day will be . . . a sixteenth? Is that how that works, you just keep
dividing?

HOWIE

I guess. And what do you mean "some day"? From your podcast,
it seems like you're . . .

DIWATA

That I'm what?

HOWIE

. . . expecting? Or . . .

DIWATA

Expecting what?

HOWIE

Aren't you . . . ?

Howie rubs his stomach.

DIWATA

Hungry?

HOWIE

Diwata . . .

DIWATA

I'm not pregnant.

HOWIE

I thought in your podcast / you said—

DIWATA

I'm not pregnant. I was drunk, if I said—

HOWIE

Really?

DIWATA

Yeah . . .

HOWIE

'Cause I work at Januzzi's, that pizza / place near—

DIWATA

Yeah, I know where it is—

HOWIE

—near the family-planning center.
   (beat)
I saw you go in there last week.

DIWATA

No, it wasn't me—

HOWIE

You had your uniform on, which . . . is kind of memorable.

Beat.

Anyway . . .
    (trying to lighten the tension)
. . . how classic is it that in a Salem strip mall you can get an
abortion and slice of pepperoni pizza in one shot, you know?

Beat.

HOWIE

Sorry, I didn't . . . I'm sorry if it's a secret or something.

DIWATA

Yeah, it is, and I was there for my friend, FYI. I wanted to be
there for her.

HOWIE

Oh . . .

DIWATA

Yeah, I can see how you would think that though—

HOWIE

Yeah, especially 'cause you went in by yourself.

DIWATA

Yeah, I was late.
    (fighting back tears)
All right sir, I'll be right back with some fries.

HOWIE

What?

Diwata exits, reenters with a plate of fries. Diwata sits down.

HOWIE

I shouldn't have said anything, I'm sorry . . .

DIWATA

I'm going back today. To that center. For—obviously . . . but . . .
have you told lots of kids? Who knows?

HOWIE

Who would I tell, I don't know anyone here. I just want to get my senior year over with, what do I care what you do? I could care less.

Howie eats a fry.

HOWIE

These are terrible.

DIWATA

They're left over from that lady's table.

Howie spits the fry into a napkin.

HOWIE

I hate Salem . . .

Diwata eats a fry.

DIWATA

Have you ever had a scare like this? With a girlfriend, or . . .

HOWIE

Uh, no. But I've never had sex with a woman.

DIWATA

Never?

HOWIE

I came out real young, when I was ten.

DIWATA

Was your first time . . . was it—

HOWIE

Uh, it was fine.

DIWATA

Yeah?

                                HOWIE

Yeah.

Beat.

                               DIWATA

Were you *ten*?

                                HOWIE

No, no, I was not ten.

                               DIWATA

Mine was fine, but a mess, you know how it is. It didn't even
go all the way in. I'm not sure it even counts, I don't know how
that works. No one tells you that.

                                HOWIE

Does your mom know, or—

                               DIWATA

If my mom knew I'd be going to hell and sitting through a lec-
ture on the rhythm method.

                                HOWIE

Where are your friends?

                               DIWATA

They're older, most of them graduated.

                                HOWIE

Where's the father?

                               DIWATA

The day after we did it, I called just to say "hey" or whatever,
and he was like, "I never would have slept with you if I wasn't
so drunk." So . . .

Beat.

                                HOWIE

So you guys are getting married?

DIWATA

(smiling)
Yeah. We're getting married in the spring.

Beat.

HOWIE

So . . . what are we going to say to Solomon?

DIWATA

Nothing. If you tell him, the Speech and Debate team will fall apart—

HOWIE

I don't care about the—I care about my reputation.

DIWATA

I care about mine. I need this, I *need* some form of performance this year that's school-sanctioned, something official for my transcript. How am I supposed to make it as an actress if I can't even find work in my own school district? I need three people to do this presentation, and you promised you'd join the team if I told you . . .

HOWIE

No, not if he wants to use my chat transcript as material!

DIWATA

I'll be the one reading it out loud . . .

HOWIE

Yeah, so—

DIWATA

I won't actually do it. Right before our presentation I'll tell him I want to switch pieces—Solomon's too nervous to present any of his stuff himself—

HOWIE

What if he isn't—

DIWATA

Then, then, we out him.

Beat.

HOWIE

If he pisses me off, I'm gonna say something . . .

DIWATA

Then I tell people what I know about you, *Blonde Boy* . . .

HOWIE

That I—what, that I'm messing around online, looking for— /
go ahead . . .

DIWATA

Looking for, for sex with older guys, yeah, well good then, you
won't be embarrassed when that gets out . . .

HOWIE

I'm gonna go . . .

DIWATA

Okay.

Howie doesn't move. Beat.

DIWATA

Did you leave yet?

Howie throws a fry at Diwata. Beat.

DIWATA

The fries aren't from anyone's table, that was a lie.

HOWIE
  (*taking a fry*)
I don't believe you but I'm starving.

DIWATA

Distract me. My appointment's in an hour. Tell me a story.

                          HOWIE
I can't think of any.

*He sees Diwata is anxious. Diwata puts her head down on the
table. Beat. Howie sighs, he can't believe he's actually going to
do this . . .*

                          HOWIE
Once upon a time, there was this kid who always wanted to
time-travel. And one day he got his wish and went all the way
back to biblical times . . .

*Howie continues the story as the lights fade to black and mysteri-
ous music fades in . . .*

SCENE 7

DUO INTERPRETATION

. . . *The mysterious musical vamp continues, coming from Diwa-ta's Casio keyboard.*

Weary from time-travel, Mary Warren, played by Diwata, enters looking more like a fat pilgrim. While it has many new frills, Diwata's waitress uniform (dyed black) forms the base of her Mary Warren costume.

Mary Warren notices Teenage Abraham Lincoln, played by Howie. He has a thin beard and perhaps a top hat.

DIWATA

(As Mary Warren)
Where am I? I must have fallen through a worm hole and traveled back in time. But to when? And to where?
(seeing Teenage Abraham Lincoln:)

Boy, whatcha doin'?
Boy, whatcha thinkin'?
Boy, what's your name?

HOWIE

(As *Teenage Abraham Lincoln*)
It's Abraham Lincoln

DIWATA

I've landed in a land
That's strange and foreign

HOWIE

Girl, tell me your name

DIWATA

It's Mary Warren
Boy, I'm from Salem
I just had my trial
They think I'm a witch
They think I'm vile
They said, girl, you'll hang, you must confess
So I lied and said, yes—I am possessed

HOWIE

You held it in?

DIWATA

I held it in

HOWIE

But Mary, you lied

DIWATA

I held it in

HOWIE

Don't you feel awful?

DIWATA

Yes, but I'm alive
(*an aside to the audience*)
This girl is headstrong
(*back to Abe*)
Abe, I lied in court

But what the heck
I lost my honor
Not my neck

The following interlude occurs over the musical vamp. Howie might have to reference a sheet of paper for the dialogue. He is wooden, uncomfortable with the text. Solomon watches in morbid fascination off to the side.

HOWIE

Wow, Mary. This makes me think twice about a talk I was going to have with my parents today.

DIWATA

What kind of talk, Abraham?

HOWIE

Oh, you know. Just, I wanted to share with them that I'm a little different. That I love them, but I also love the way the army men look in and out of their uniforms, that kind of stuff.

DIWATA

You want my advice, Abraham?

HOWIE

Yes, Mary Warren.

She resumes the song, in full belt.

DIWATA

Hold it in

HOWIE

I shouldn't tell them?

DIWATA

Not on your life
Hold it in

HOWIE

But they'll still love me

DIWATA

Boy, get a wife
(*an aside to the audience*)
A sexy lady
(*back to Abe*)
Don't you want to run the country some day?

HOWIE

Yes—you think I can do it?

DIWATA

Not if you're gay

HOWIE

But I'm bright I'm moral
I could win

DIWATA

Trust me, I'm a Puritan

HOWIE

I'll hold it in

DIWATA

Hold it in
Keep your feelings inside
Hold it in

HOWIE

(*riffing*)
Girl, I can't lie . . .

DIWATA

Boy, swallow your pride

(*upset, breaking character, to Howie*)
Please don't riff . . .

HOWIE

If I hold it in
I lose my bravery

DIWATA

If you hold it in
You will end slavery
You win

HOWIE

I win

DIWATA AND HOWIE

If you (I) hold it in

Beat. Teenage Abe and Marry Warren hold hands. Diwata nods to Solomon, indicating that this is his cue. Solomon addresses the audience, reading from an index card. The musical vamp continues in the background. Diwata has every line of Solomon's speech (which she wrote) memorized. Occasionally, she unintentionally mouths the words.

SOLOMON
(reading)
Two teenagers . . . lost . . . separated by different times, yet united in their quest to speak their minds. Far-fetched? Perhaps. But far from true?—far from it.

Solomon doesn't understand what he just read. He looks to Diwata. She urges him to continue while trying not to break her character/pose. Solomon rolls his eyes, continues.

SOLOMON
Teenagers today are holding lots of things inside. Feelings, fears, and guns.

Mary Warren hikes up her skirt to reveal a gun attached to her leg.

SOLOMON
(reading)
But by keeping things hidden inside, who are kids really helping? Themselves? Or the adults who would rather ignore uncomfortable subjects rather than engage them. After all, do we live in Salem, Oregon, or Salem, Massachusetts, circa sixteen insert the date of whenever the witches were burned?

Solomon, perplexed, turns to Diwata who stares daggers at him, once again urging him to continue. Frustrated, he continues.

SOLOMON

Puritanism seems to be lingering in our country. So I ask: would Mary Warren's naked forest-dancing be any more welcome today? Let's find out.

Beat. He reads.

SOLOMON

At this point, all three of us strip down to nude bodystockings and begin naked forest-dancing—
    (*to Diwata*)
Okay, I'm sorry, no way, no way—

Solomon tears the index card up.

HOWIE

A nude bodystocking? You're a dumbass, Diwata.

Diwata turns the music off.

DIWATA

It will be tasteful if you guys can commit. Trust me.

HOWIE

What's a nude bodystocking?

DIWATA

I can show you mine—

SOLOMON

No, stop. *Stop.* I agreed to participate, but there will be no naked forest-dancing in the presentation. This is from your musical, isn't it?

DIWATA

It also falls within the rules of "Group Interpretation"—

(reading from the rule book)
—"'Group Interpretation' is just that—the group interpretation of a narrative. Material may be original. Costumes, props, visual aids . . . prohibited." Shit, so we lose the costumes . . .

SOLOMON

The costumes aren't the problem. It's the material.

DIWATA

When Howie told me the stories you guys wrote as kids, I realized that they were the missing link to the story *I've* been trying to write. Mary Warren *time-travels* . . .

SOLOMON

Oh my God . . .

DIWATA

. . . she meets various figures in American history: Abe Lincoln, Martin Luther King, Jr., Idina Menzel—

SOLOMON

I never gave you permission to use my story—

DIWATA

You can't trademark Teenage Abraham Lincoln, and as Team Captain . . .

SOLOMON

Self-appointed Team Captain . . .

DIWATA

(over the above line)
. . . I think it's important for the school board to see us working together for at least one category. And "Group Interpretation" is a way for us to do that, to tell a story together.

SOLOMON

Then we do it, but we come up with material that we each have a hand in creating.

HOWIE

Can we please get this over with? Please.

DIWATA

Fine. We will do "Group Interpretation" together, material TBD for the category AKA "GI sans Joe," you know, hot flow—

SOLOMON   HOWIE

Yo ho, I know.   Yo ho, yo ho, I know.

SOLOMON

Moving on . . .

DIWATA

Moving on . . . as Team Captain—

SOLOMON

Self-appointed Team / Captain . . .

DIWATA

—I would like to—I'm not acknowledging those remarks—I would like to do a check-in with all of the members of the team and get a progress report. Can we all get in a circle? Please? Thanks.

Howie and Solomon look at each other, sigh, and stand together to form a circle.

SOLOMON

This is a triangle.

DIWATA

(ignoring Solomon)
Howie, can we have an update? You agreed to cover the category of "Declamation."

HOWIE

Right. Well, I'll find a speech, no problem. That's it. Please move on. Please.

DIWATA

And Solomon?

SOLOMON

Well, Diwata was helping me do "Original Oratory"—

DIWATA

"Double-O," yes . . .

SOLOMON

My plan was to have you read the article I wrote about, you
know—the mayor and Mr. Healy and—

HOWIE

I can't wait to read that.

SOLOMON

Are you being sarcastic?—

DIWATA

He's being difficult. Howie's just nervous about how he will
come off in all of this—

SOLOMON

No, don't worry . . . that's why . . . I'd like to have some other
material precede the speech . . . I'd like to use Howie's transcript.

DIWATA

I don't understand—you want me to read BiGuy and Blonde
Boy's chat first?—

SOLOMON

No, I want to showcase it myself using a different category—
"Poetry Reading."

HOWIE

How?

SOLOMON

I think it needs to be visual. I'm a wizard with PowerPoint,
I could project the chat, and suddenly it's in its original form—
it becomes physical, it's cyber-poetry, more importantly, it's
indisputable . . . it's closer to real reporting, it's evidence . . .

HOWIE

This isn't a trial.

DIWATA

Yeah, and as proud as I am that you've learned about a new category, especially since Howie has never shown that kind of Speech spirit, the rules say you're not allowed to use audio-visual.

SOLOMON

So we break the rules, the material itself will cause enough controversy, right?

HOWIE

I don't know . . .

SOLOMON

And we can have some music underscoring it—something ordinary to show that you're just some common kid—an ordinary boy who found himself in extraordinary circumstances.
(to Howie)
So no one will think you're a freak.

HOWIE

Speak for yourself.

SOLOMON

What? What's that supposed to mean?

HOWIE

You keep looking at me all weird, like you hate me, like—

SOLOMON

What? You obviously have those feelings, not me—

DIWATA

Okay, time out.

HOWIE

You're so . . . you're obsessed with being normal, you're so . . .

DIWATA

Let's move on, please . . .

SOLOMON

I'm so what? Tell me. What / am I?

HOWIE

All of your shirts have *alligators* on them, you're—it's like you're always in costume—

SOLOMON

I like my shirts, they—

HOWIE

You don't even have a personality, / you're so . . .

SOLOMON

—and it's a *crocodile*, it's a *crocodile*, so . . .

HOWIE

I *hate* the way you act, it makes me sick.

Beat.

DIWATA
  (as if nothing harsh has been said, calmly contributing to the conversation)
I hate when people use too much vibrato. When they're belting.

She turns to Solomon.

DIWATA

Your turn.

SOLOMON
  (to Diwata)
You're not funny.

Howie is pissed. Awkward silence.

DIWATA

Okay . . . now that that's settled . . . next order of business is . . .
and, I'm not sure if I already told you guys already, but . . . yeah,
so I called that reporter Solomon's dad knows—the one from
the *Oregonian*, and . . .

SOLOMON

Diwata, why would you—

DIWATA

. . . I'm talking, thanks, and she wants to come and meet with
us before our presentation—do some sort of human-interest
story on the formation of our Speech and Debate team. It's not
a big deal—

SOLOMON	HOWIE
She's *my* contact— You shouldn't have called her without telling me first—	No way, we're not having some reporter talk to us

DIWATA

It would just be about—I'd perform, you'd smile for ten minutes, it's good publicity for us—

SOLOMON

You're not performing, she's *my* contact—if she comes we're
going to discuss *my* work, maybe I even—I'd have to break my
story, to tell her about Healy . . .

HOWIE

What? No way—

DIWATA

No—she'll steal the story and write it herself, we still save that
for the presentation . . .

SOLOMON

I know but I've been, I keep thinking maybe people should
know *now*—like it's our responsibility to tell people . . .

HOWIE

But what has he done? I'm legal in the state of Oregon, so what's the big deal? Have you even ever *had* sex?

SOLOMON

Oh, well, now you're going off on a tangent . . .

HOWIE

I'm just trying to understand why you're obsessed with stories of sexual misconduct. You started with the mayor, then when you learned about me and / Mr. Healy—

SOLOMON

I'm not obsessed, and they're related, so, like any good reporter, I pursued the story—

HOWIE

Is it newsworthy?

SOLOMON

Yes, the mayor's personal life is fair game because it conflicts with his public policy.

HOWIE

So that's the mayor, Mr. Healy isn't / a politician—

SOLOMON

I think his online behavior conflicts with what people in this town expect from a public schoolteacher, Howie. Do you disagree with that? How can you disagree with that?

DIWATA

All right, calm down, ladies—

HOWIE

He didn't know I lived in Salem and—you're right, fine, yes— the whole thing is—I'm embarrassed about it okay? But it's private. Just because you know about it doesn't make you entitled to broadcast it.

SOLOMON

I disagree. What if he hurts another student?

HOWIE

Who did he hurt?

Solomon walks away.

HOWIE

Who did he hurt!?

SOLOMON

Stop yelling at me, I don't know!

DIWATA

Solomon, return to the circle please.

HOWIE

We're not meeting with her—

SOLOMON

It's not your decision.

HOWIE

Of course it is, I'm the one who will look like a freak!

SOLOMON

You should have thought about that before you had that chat.

Beat.

SOLOMON

My dad's waiting for me outside, I gotta go.

Solomon exits. Blackout.

SCENE 8

DECLAMATION

Howie stands at the front of the room, reading from a piece of paper. Solomon and Diwata watch. Howie directs his speech at Solomon.

HOWIE

(reading)

"As mayor of Salem, I want to sincerely apologize to you for the shame I have brought to the city and to my office. This week the *Statesman Journal* reported that I have visited a gay chat line on the internet and had relationships with adult men. I don't deny that."

SOLOMON

What are you reading? —Is this supposed to be your speech?—

HOWIE

Why don't you let me finish.

(continuing)
"I have always considered a person's private life private and have respected others in this way. I intended to keep my private life private as well. And I apologize. I do ask one thing if you are willing. Since my cancer I've taken to prayer and believe it has healing power. Please pray for me."

DIWATA
(to Solomon)
That's from today's paper.

HOWIE
The mayor sent this in an email to all city employees.

SOLOMON
Declamation is usually the reading of a speech that's acclaimed, like, the Gettysburg Address or something. Not a public statement that has no literary or historical value.

HOWIE
At least he was man enough to apologize.

SOLOMON
Is that an apology?

HOWIE
That's why it's so sad, I mean, the man's already dead. His career's probably over and even then, he can barely bring himself to tell the truth—even when he's backed into a corner. It's awful.

SOLOMON
It's awful that he would bring up his cancer. I mean, where was his cancer while he was cruising the web for barely articulate eighteen-year-old boys? And the part about adult relationships, that's a lie—just because the kids were legal he's calling them adult relationships.

HOWIE
Don't you think a lot of successful, powerful straight guys would spend time with teenage girls if they had the chance, if the girls were willing?

SOLOMON

No, I don't know, not if they were good people, and what's with your euphemisms—"spend time with teenage girls," that's a bit glossy, don't you think? You're not even capable of saying what you really mean.

HOWIE

Are you gay?

Diwata looks away.

HOWIE

Are you?

Awful silence. Throughout the following exchange, Solomon does not lose his cool or indicate anything is wrong.

SOLOMON

What is this? Who are you talking to?

DIWATA

Solomon, we don't really care, it's just—if you are—

SOLOMON

What?
   (*beat*)
If I am, it's none of your business. What is this?
   (*beat*)
It's none of your business.

HOWIE

According to you it is. It conflicts with your public—

SOLOMON

That's politics, that's—I have no—I'm not in politics, what is this, if you don't talk to me I'm leaving, what is this?

HOWIE

It's hypocritical if you're—

SOLOMON

And hypocrisy, *if* I was hypocritical, it would be irrelevant—

HOWIE

So you *are* hypocritical, then? What does that mean?

SOLOMON

What do you want me to say?

HOWIE

I want to know if you're gay.

Again, Solomon remains cool.

SOLOMON

Why? What, is this because today I changed the style of my shirt? Huh?
(*trying to lighten the tension*)
I told you this would happen—I took your advice, dressed a little different and look, you're already assuming I'm gay. C'mon, guys, what is this?

Beat.

DIWATA

It was me in the third floor bathroom last year—I saw you and Mr. Healy, I was the one in the stall.

Solomon looks to both of them for an explanation.

HOWIE

If you use anything you know about us without our permission, we will tell people what we know about you. I'd like all the copies of our conversation back too, the transcripts you have.

Beat.

SOLOMON

What did she tell you? Because—I don't even know what—what is this all about?

Solomon . . .

SOLOMON

No, I'm just saying I don't even know what you're talking about.

Diwata and Howie aren't sure how to proceed.

DIWATA

Solomon, it's not a big deal . . .

SOLOMON

What did you see?

DIWATA

We're not going to tell anyone. Howie, tell him. We won't tell anyone.

SOLOMON

Oh, okay. Whatever. Sure. I don't even know what this is about.

Beat.

DIWATA

I saw you.

SOLOMON

Whatever. I've got to go.

Solomon starts to cough. He goes to the wastebasket. He throws up.

DIWATA

Oh my God . . .

Solomon keeps coughing, throws up again.

HOWIE
(*to Diwata, unsure of what else to say or do*)
Are there any paper towels in here, or . . .

Diwata gets some tissues. Howie is frozen. Solomon sits by the garbage can, not looking at them. Beat.

DIWATA
(still keeping her distance from Solomon)
No one knows, I just told Howie . . .

Solomon can't look at either of them. He buries his head, faces away.

Diwata and Howie are unsure of what to do.

SOLOMON
(angrily)
Do I have to say something to you?

Howie and Diwata attempt to say something once or twice but stop. The whole experience is tense, awful, and quiet. A very, very long beat.

Diwata looks to Howie, then cautiously approaches Solomon, unsure.

DIWATA
I lost my virginity with my sweatshirt on.

HOWIE
What?

DIWATA
(to Howie)
I feel bad, he looks like he's gonna kill himself, so I'm just saying . . .
(to Solomon)
No one knows that, I never told anyone that.

HOWIE
Jesus Christ . . . leave him alone.

DIWATA

(*to Solomon*)
I was home, a little drunk on my mom's bed, and . . .

HOWIE

Oh my God . . .

DIWATA

. . . when it started, and I don't even remember how it all started,
but it was happening and my pants were around my ankles . . .

HOWIE

Oh my God . . .

DIWATA

. . . wearing this lame sweatshirt I didn't even like, it was a hand-
me-down from my cousin, I had to throw it away, I couldn't look
at it after it was over. My mom found it in the garbage, and she
was like—"Diwata, we need to give this to Goodwill if you're
not going to wear it. You know we don't throw clothes out."
(*beat*)
I could have at least had a nice one on. I have a Champion
sweatshirt I like, something nicer.

Beat. To Solomon.

DIWATA

I won't tell anyone. I promise.

Beat.

DIWATA

(*to Howie*)
Your turn.

HOWIE

Oh my God.

DIWATA

Do it.

Beat.

HOWIE

I'm in love with Diwata.

DIWATA

How much do I hate you. I hate you so much.

Diwata smacks Howie. Beat.

To Solomon—sincere, but not sentimental. Howie doesn't feel sorry for himself.

HOWIE

That dance I made up, for the Boy Scouts talent show—I said I left before I could embarrass myself. Well, I *did* teach them the dance. And all the kids—guys younger than me laughed. The leaders all laughed, and—they did this thing where they tried to *hide* the fact that they were laughing—they were like shifting their weight, looking away so I couldn't see them smiling when—I could tell, obviously. And then they said we didn't have time to learn all of it, when—there was at least fifteen minutes left. It was really bad. The kids called me "Miss Gay B.S.A." So . . .

Beat.

DIWATA

B.S.A.—bathing-suit areas?

HOWIE

No, dumbass. Boy Scouts of America.

DIWATA

You know, Mary Warren got in trouble for dancing naked in the forest with Tituba. It's nothing to be ashamed of.

HOWIE

You are such a dumbass, Diwata.

DIWATA

You are totally teaching me your moves.

HOWIE

Jesus Christ . . .

DIWATA

. . . and oh my God, I'm getting some killer ideas for our "Group Interpretation" performance. Do you guys want to hear them?

SOLOMON	HOWIE
No, of course not . . .	No, not now . . .

DIWATA

When?

HOWIE

(gesturing toward Solomon, who still has his head buried in his hands by the garbage can)
Diwata . . .

DIWATA

Howard, no—my team, my chance to perform has taken a consistent back seat to all of your homo-drama, so let's just be clear. You're both doing this. You're not walking away from this team. Promise . . .

HOWIE

Diwata . . .

DIWATA

And I decide the material we perform for "Group Interpretation." No crapping all over my ideas like you did last time, otherwise we'll never agree. Promise. *Promise.*

SOLOMON	HOWIE
No, I'm not doing it—not unless you promise that none of this leaves this room.	Whatever shuts you up. One presentation, one performance, then we're done.

                              DIWATA
I'm really moved by our team spirit.

                               HOWIE
What is that smell?

                              SOLOMON
My vomit.

                              DIWATA
So nasty . . .

                               HOWIE
    (to Solomon)
Are you going to come out to your parents?

                              SOLOMON
Stop it, Howie. You think you know me. They already know, did
you know that? No, so . . .

                               HOWIE
Huh?

                              SOLOMON
I know you guys think you're some sort of private eyes, breaking the story . . .

                               HOWIE
Well you never said you were gay.

                              SOLOMON
. . . last summer my parents found me this camp . . .

                              DIWATA
They know? Your parents know?

                              SOLOMON
. . . which, for the first time addressed those gay issues . . .

                              DIWATA
Like musical-theater camp?

SOLOMON

No . . .

HOWIE

What issues? You're gay, who cares? It's not an issue—

SOLOMON

—no it's this, like a ministry group for kids who are, you know, like me, but who . . .

HOWIE

Jesus . . .

DIWATA

Let him talk . . .

SOLOMON

. . . who want to live a life free of . . . kids who don't want to live the gay lifestyle. Who don't want to be promiscuous and stuff . . .

HOWIE

Gay people don't have to be promiscuous, I can't believe you'd say that!

SOLOMON

Stop yelling at me—

HOWIE

She's *deranged*, that doesn't mean all *straight* people are . . .

DIWATA

Excuse me, *Blonde Boy*?

SOLOMON

She doesn't go around sleeping with people she meets online.

DIWATA

I'm right here . . .

HOWIE

I don't do that, Solomon!

DIWATA

Then why are you surfing for sex all the time—

HOWIE

Why did you get drunk at a party, get knocked up and spend an afternoon at an abortion clinic—

DIWATA

Howie!

SOLOMON

I *knew* you were pregnant!

DIWATA

(*to Howie*)
How could you say that?

HOWIE

I'm sorry—

SOLOMON

You had an abortion?

DIWATA

Shut your mouth about it, you shut your mouth.

SOLOMON

I can't belie—

DIWATA

Shuttup!

Beat.

HOWIE

So I guess . . . what happens now?

DIWATA

I don't know. Let's . . . I don't know . . .

SOLOMON

What you saw in the bathroom . . . it wasn't what you think . . .

DIWATA

Okay, but I saw . . . then, okay, *you* tell me, what happened?

SOLOMON

It wasn't—I wasn't hurt or anything . . .

HOWIE

But . . . okay, so . . .

SOLOMON

I don't know if . . . maybe, I think, you'll laugh . . .

HOWIE

I won't laugh . . .

SOLOMON

. . . but as a guy, I don't know if . . . maybe I lost my, you know,
virginity . . . I don't know . . .

Diwata smiles. Howie laughs quietly.

DIWATA

Uh, okay, I would have seen that. Trust me.

HOWIE

   (*trying not to laugh*)
No, it's not your virginity, bud, I doubt he went that far.

SOLOMON

Not in the bathroom.

Howie and Diwata are caught off guard.

SOLOMON

No, no, no—he didn't hurt me—

Knocking at the door.

HOWIE
(overlapping)
Solomon, if he—

SOLOMON
Really. He didn't hurt me, never . . .

More knocking.

VOICE
(from outside)
Hello . . . ? Can I come in?

SOLOMON
This doesn't leave this room, okay? This doesn't leave this room . . .

The Reporter enters.

REPORTER
Hello . . . oh, hi, guys. I'm sorry, sorry to interrupt. Hi. I'm Jan Clark, from the *Oregonian*. I'm sorry to interrupt. Hi, Solomon. Can I just sit down and observe?

Long beat. Solomon, Diwata, and Howie are shocked. They look at each other, unsure of what to say. They are a collective mess.

REPORTER
A friend of yours, a . . . Diwanda, we spoke last week. She's been leaving me voicemails asking if I'd stop by one of your rehearsals and . . . your dad, Solomon, he mentioned you were here rehearsing, so . . .
(beat)
He said he'd call you on your cell to tell you I was coming.

SOLOMON
My cell was turned off.

REPORTER
Well please, just pretend I'm not here. I'll just sit and observe if that's all right.

Beat.

SOLOMON

The three of us were just practicing Lincoln-Douglas debate.

DIWATA

(to Solomon)
Lincoln-Douglas is two people.

HOWIE

Would you be able to come back at another time? We're working out some rough spots, you know?

REPORTER

Oh. Well . . .

SOLOMON

Yeah, I'm sorry, it's just, we're just a mess right now.

REPORTER

Is there a particular rehearsal I should attend, or . . . ?

DIWATA

You should come back and see us do "Group Interpretation."

REPORTER

What's "Group Interpretation"?

DIWATA

It's a category in which all three of us come together to tell a story. It's the only one we do together.

REPORTER

What story will you be telling?

HOWIE   SOLOMON

Not now . . .   No, Diwata . . .

DIWATA

We can tell any story we like, a fairy tale, a fable, a legend . . . but we've decided to tell *our* story. The story of how we came together.

REPORTER

Well, that's the story I'm hoping to capture. I cover the regional beat on the local NPR station—this is exactly the kind of story they love to air.

DIWATA

You mean it would be read on the radio? Amazing . . .

REPORTER

Well, not so amazing—it would just be me reading a shortened version of the article I'd put together for the *Oregonian*.

DIWATA

Could I read it? I'm amazing at voice-overs.

REPORTER

Well, no—the journalists read their own reports—

DIWATA

I could *play* you. Could I play you?

SOLOMON

No, / Diwata.

HOWIE

Diwata, pull back.

REPORTER

I'm hoping to get this in the Sunday broadcast, so, the sooner you guys can tell me your story the better.

DIWATA

It's going to be pretty controversial, just to warn you.

SOLOMON

Diwata . . .

DIWATA

(to Solomon)
I didn't tell her anything . . .

REPORTER

What's controversial about it?

Howie jumps in before Diwata can speak.

HOWIE

The rules of "Group Interpretation" say that you can't use costumes or props.
 (beat)
And we use costumes and props.
 (beat)
And that's going to be pretty controversial.

REPORTER

I see.

DIWATA

Dancing isn't allowed either, but I simply couldn't resist using
the very special dance moves that Howard is going to teach us.

HOWIE

Jesus Christ . . .

REPORTER

What type of dance?

DIWATA

Striptease. Mainly.
 (aside, to Solomon)
I still have my bodystocking.

Solomon buries his head in his hands.

REPORTER

 (laughing)
That does sound controversial. And what is the significance of
all this dancing?

DIWATA

Well Jan, besides finally having a platform for my ten years
of jazz/modern dance—the significance of the striptease is to
show that, as we shed our clothing, we are bearing, via meta-

phorical conceit . . . bearing our . . . bathing-suit areas, which is the term from stranger-danger, the one they use in place of penis and vagina. The piece is inspired by each of our original flows—a mashing together of each of our voices.

HOWIE

Mostly hers.

REPORTER

(*taking out her notepad*)
And so, explain to me the whole bathing-suit business again?

SOLOMON

She means, it's like, we're showing people that ready or not—

DIWATA

Here come our bathing-suit areas.

SOLOMON

(*aside, to Diwata*)
Please don't talk.
(*to the Reporter*)
We're showing people that ready or not, we're going to discuss things that are affecting us in real terms, adult terms, and we won't apologize even if it makes you uncomfortable.

HOWIE

And my moves aren't that special. Just a disclaimer.

DIWATA

He's just nervous people will laugh at him. Childhood trauma.

SOLOMON

(*to the Reporter*)
I'm really sorry about this . . .

REPORTER

Not at all, this is quite good timing, really—I'm writing a new foreword to my book—it deals with adolescence, how kids like you often form your own clusters apart from adults; and the formation of your group—I think it would be the perfect new beginning, capturing the image of you three performing this group event—what is it called?

DIWATA

"Group Interpretation."

REPORTER

Could I stop by sometime before Friday? Just to see even a rough rehearsal? You'd be doing me a huge favor. I'd speak to your parents of course to make sure this was okay.

DIWATA

What do we get out of it?

SOLOMON

Diwata . . .
    (to the Reporter)
I'm sorry.

REPORTER

It's fine, it's a fair question.
    (beat)
Other than an appearance in the *Oregonian*, I'm not sure what else I have to offer.

Beat.

DIWATA

Is your sister-in-law still on the board of the Salem Dinner Theater? I googled you, so . . . sorry if that's weird.

SOLOMON

Yes, it is weird, Diwata.

HOWIE

She's an actress.

REPORTER

I could certainly introduce you, if you like.

SOLOMON

That isn't necessary, we're not asking you for any favors.

HOWIE

Do you know anyone in town who might be willing to serve as an advisor for the gay-straight alliance at school? I've been looking for someone for over a month, but . . .

SOLOMON

Howie . . .

REPORTER

Well, certainly no promises, but I might be able to help.

SOLOMON

Again, there's no way we could be ready in time.

REPORTER

Solomon, your father told me about the article you wrote for the school paper. No promises, but there's a chance we could find a place for it in the *Oregonian*.

All three look at each other.

Introduction to George Michael's "Freedom" sounds.

Blackout.

SCENE 9

GROUP INTERPRETATION

The music continues from the previous scene.

The dance should primarily be just that—a choreographed dance, with dance moves. It should loosely convey the following story:

Diwata enters, "dances" her blog using some very basic jazz/modern dance moves. She is totally serious about all of this.

Howie enters, somewhat reluctantly, and after receiving a signal from Diwata, does some of his very special moves. Diwata joins in.

Howie and Diwata look for Solomon to enter. He doesn't. Diwata exits, quickly returns pushing Solomon onstage.

Howie and Solomon flank Diwata and each pull one of her arms—they are fighting for control of her. They move one way, then move the other way—Diwata is very dramatic about all of this.

Diwata does a grand move (i.e., a lift, or stage-diving from a desk into the boys' arms). It's awkward for the boys, but she maintains full stage presence. Her moves grow in intensity and difficulty, and it becomes clear she has choreographed the dance to make herself the center of attention. She uses the boys as tools for her more complex moves.

And then, in time with the music . . .

Diwata removes a piece of clothing.

And then another.

And another.

Diwata is wearing nothing but a nude bodystocking. She is in heaven.

Howie and Solomon follow her lead, removing their clothing, a bit less enthusiastically. Howie is getting a kick out of the proceedings . . . and even Solomon relaxes (just a bit) as the music reaches its infectious climax.

The boys have on poorly dyed flesh-colored baggy T-shirts and boxers.

With a flourish, they finish. A tympani/cymbal crash sounds in time with a sharp blackout.

SCENE 10

ORAL INTERPRETATION OF PROSE

Howie, Solomon, and Diwata are each in their bedrooms, listening to the radio broadcast.

RADIO HOST
(voice-over)
The mayor may not be granting interviews, but three local students are talking about the biggest political scandal in Oregon's history. The newly formed Speech and Debate team at North Salem High School, led by team captain Diwanda Jones—

SOLOMON
Team captain?

DIWATA
Diwanda?

RADIO HOST

(voice-over)

—is attempting to explore the ins and outs of the sex scandal and other taboo topics using the various Speech and Debate categories in unconventional and creative ways . . .

SOLOMON

Good, solid . . .

RADIO HOST

(voice-over)

Regional Beat reporter Jan Clark sat in on a recent rehearsal of the team and had a chance to speak with Salem's young oratorical pioneers.

REPORTER

(voice-over)

The rehearsal I attended was anything but ordinary . . .

DIWATA

That's right . . .

REPORTER

(voice-over)

Up first was a wild dance fantasia in which the kids removed their clothing to reveal that each of them was wearing beige undergarments . . .

DIWATA

(disappointed)

She didn't get the metaphor . . . oh, Jan . . .

REPORTER

(voice-over)

. . . a self-professed symbol of their struggles to bear their souls to an adult community who rarely takes the time to listen . . .

HOWIE

Please call her "Diwanda" again. Please . . .

REPORTER
(voice-over)
A more detailed description of the scene will make an appearance in the new foreword to my book, *Adolescents Alone*, now in its eighth printing at Simon & Schuster.

DIWATA
She's plugging her book?

REPORTER
(voice-over)
As I note in my book . . .
(Diwata gives the radio the finger)
. . . kids of this generation have a tendency to search out a safe place, an escape from their loneliness, forming small complex clusters of friends to help navigate the complex world of high school together.

SOLOMON
Friends?

DIWATA
No, we're not—

REPORTER
(voice-over)
. . . even as I wandered North Salem's hall's, I was hit with my own fears and insecurities. I was also hit with the frighteningly familiar smells of the cafeteria, that odd scent of Pine-sol mingling with rotting food . . .

SOLOMON
That would be my vomit.

REPORTER
(voice-over)
. . . and as I sat in the classroom, I was once again reminded of the simple truth: adolescents crave meaningful relationships with adults who care about them.

                    VOICE (DIWATA'S MOTHER)
Diwata . . .

                              DIWATA
    (yelling)
Mother, please die so you will be dead. *God.*

                            REPORTER
    (*voice-over*)
That is an oversimplification of my own argument, which is
thoroughly fleshed out in my book, *Adolescents Alone*, published by Simon & Schuster.

                              DIWATA
Stop plugging your book, Jan.

                            REPORTER
    (*voice-over*)
And as for Solomon, Howard, and Diwanda . . .

                              DIWATA
Oh, c'mon!

                              HOWIE
    (*loving the mistake*)
Yes . . .

                            REPORTER
    (*voice-over*)
. . . at present, their work may not be particularly groundbreak-
ing . . .

                    HOWIE/DIWATA/SOLOMON
Ouch/bitch/owww . . .

                            REPORTER
    (*voice-over*)
. . . and if their writing or performing does not show prodigious
skill . . .

HOWIE/DIWATA/SOLOMON
Ouch/slut/ohhhh . . .

REPORTER
(*voice-over*)

. . . someday soon this dynamic trio will be ready to share their performance with us; and when they are, I encourage you to show up with an open mind. If you go to listen, you will leave talking.

RADIO HOST
(*voice-over*)

Jan Clark will be reading from her book, *Adolescents Alone*, at Barnes & Noble this Saturday at one P.M.

HOWIE/SOLOMON
Pathetic . . . /Unbelievable . . .

DIWATA
Media Whore . . .

Blackout.

SCENE 11

STUDENT CONGRESS

A sign that reads WELCOME TO THE FIRST MEETING OF NORTH SALEM'S GAY/STRAIGHT ALLIANCE!

Howie, Diwata, and Solomon are seated. They look toward the door, their silence upstaged by the sign.

Howie checks to see if anyone else is coming.

DIWATA
How weird is it if we are the only members of the Speech and Debate team *and* the gay/straight alliance?

Howie throws something at Diwata.

HOWIE
It's already after three, I guess we should start. First on the agenda is meet-and-greet, introductions.

SOLOMON

Hi, I'm Solomon . . .

DIWATA

Oh, hi—we actually met in the third floor bathroom last year . . .

HOWIE

Okay, enough . . .

SOLOMON

That's disgusting.

HOWIE

I'm sure more people will come once the word gets out.

SOLOMON

My parents think I'm doing community service.

DIWATA

How are Mary and Joseph?

SOLOMON

That's not funny.

Beat.

SOLOMON

We've got, like, a family therapist now, so . . .

HOWIE

That's some progress, yes?

SOLOMON

Uh, some, yeah . . .

DIWATA

(*raising her hand*)
Oh, oh—can I put something on the agenda—the dates I'm
going on for the Salem Dinner Theater production of *Fiddler
on the Roof*? The theater is gay-friendly, it's relevant.

HOWIE

That's fine, Diwata.

SOLOMON

How's that going?

DIWATA

I'm the standby for all the daughters. I have to serve drinks at intermission right now, which sucks, but I'm going on on the twentieth. Shprintze is having her wisdom teeth out.

SOLOMON

Nice.

HOWIE

Duly noted—

Loud knocking on the door.

HOWIE

Come on in . . .

Howie goes to the door, looks.

HOWIE

There's no one there. That's weird.

DIWATA

Ohmigod, we have a gay ghost. I love it.

HOWIE

It's Mr. Healy, haunting us . . .

SOLOMON

That's not funny.

DIWATA

Healy's come to offer handjobs to all incoming students.

SOLOMON

Stop it.

More knocking at the door.

SOLOMON

Come in!

VOICE #1	VOICE #2
(from offstage)	*(from offstage)*
You guys want to give me	Fucking faggots!
head, cocksuckers! . . .	

From offstage the sound of laughter and kids running away. Beat. Howie goes to the door, looks.

HOWIE

It's your mom and dad, Solomon.

Diwata finds this hilarious.

SOLOMON

Do you think—you don't think they heard what we were talking about, do you?

DIWATA

No, no—

HOWIE

We didn't say anything specific about Mr. Healy, we just—no, I'm sure we didn't.

SOLOMON

Diwata said about—you heard what she said.

DIWATA

No one would know what that meant, it was a generic remark, God.

Beat.

SOLOMON

Well . . . should we keep going, or . . . ?

Yes, what's next?

HOWIE

Election of officers. There are four positions open, so . . . guess we save that for next meeting, when the word spreads.

SOLOMON

Definitely.

HOWIE

And that's it.

SOLOMON

Okay.

DIWATA

Good.

HOWIE

Meeting adjourned.

DIWATA

I gotta go upload another video podcast to my website before 'mah fans get upset . . .

HOWIE

Your last one had, like, three hits.

DIWATA

All viral videos start from a small place, Howard. Later, ladies . . .

Diwata exits.

HOWIE

They didn't hear us.

SOLOMON

You don't know that.

HOWIE

What if they did? I mean . . . what if they did?

SOLOMON

I don't know what she saw . . . I don't know if Diwata told you
details or . . . if she said I was the one who, you know . . .

HOWIE

What does it matter?

SOLOMON

Yeah, well . . . because I'm not telling people that.

Howie begins to gather his things.

SOLOMON

Hey, maybe we could hang out sometime, like for real, you know?

HOWIE

As friends, yeah—of course—

SOLOMON

Sure, of course as friends. Of course as *friends*.

HOWIE

I think it's clear you need a Christian hottie, you know?

SOLOMON

Dude, of course. Yes. Cool. I'm gonna find like a million in youth
group, / now that I'm out . . .

HOWIE

No, I know, I know.

SOLOMON

Definitely, awesome then. Well then, really cool then, we'll talk
soon.

Howie sees Solomon is defeated—calls to him before he can exit.

HOWIE

Yeah, and I did go to the park that night to meet Healy.

Howie finishes gathering his things, and starts to exit.

SOLOMON

You said you didn't.

HOWIE

I didn't meet him . . . but . . . because he never showed up.
Guess he didn't like my pic. I shouldn't have said I was a blonde.
    (stops, sees Solomon isn't smiling)
I'm kidding.

SOLOMON

So—

HOWIE

I'm just telling you, I don't want to talk about it.

SOLOMON

No. Me neither.

Howie exits. Blackout.

SCENE 12

ORIGINAL ORATORY

Diwata is alone in her bedroom creating her latest podcast. Music underscores her speech.

DIWATA

Right now, the overture is striking up for North Salem High's final dress rehearsal of *Once Upon a Mattress*. Sadly, I am not participating in this year's show due to miscasting. For weeks now, I pondered revenge, especially after meeting two lovely young ladies, two girly fans who loved my blog . . .

Lights up on Howie and Solomon in separate rooms listening to her blog broadcast with headphones.

HOWIE	SOLOMON
Oh, she's dead.	I'm going to kill her . . .

DIWATA

. . . but then I stopped and asked myself: Diwata, what would Jesus do? What would Mary do? And then I thought . . .

(she stops the music)
. . . what would Mary *Rodgers* do?

She starts the music again, turns up the volume on her Casio keyboard. A funkier vamp continues under the following . . .

DIWATA

I wondered: what would the organization in charge of licensing the rights to *Once Upon a Mattress* do? So I called and asked them. Imagine my surprise when I was informed that if any changes were made to the script without proper consent . . . a representative from the Rodgers & Hammerstein organization would fly out, see the show; and if what I reported proved to be correct . . . the show would be shut down.

Howie and Solomon react.

HOWIE

No, she didn't . . .

DIWATA

This is all purely hypothetical, of course.
(beat)
Still . . . if I were you, I wouldn't buy my tickets in advance. Rest in peace Mary . . . whether it be in a grave or on your living room couch. This flow's for you.
(singing:)

Oh . . . oh . . .

Sing it with me now . . .

Howie and Solomon sing along with the broadcast, singing with Diwata.

HOWIE

Oh . . . oh . . .

                    DIWATA AND SOLOMON
(simultaneous with Howie)
Oh-ee, oh-ee . . .

                          DIWATA
Take it home now . . .

    Yadda-da-da . . .

                          SOLOMON
(simultaneous with above)
Oh-ee . . . oh-ee . . .

                          HOWIE
(simultaneous with above)
Oh . . . oh . . .

                    VOICE (DIWATA'S MOTHER)
Hey, hey, hey . . . keep it down.

Diwata turns her Casio off; the singing stops.

                          DIWATA
Signing off for the last time. Good night.

The lights fade on Diwata.

                          HOWIE
G'night . . .

The lights fade on Howie.

Solomon is alone in his bedroom in front of his laptop. He types a message. It is projected as in the first scene. His screen name is "Abe16."

ABE16   im new to this chat room
ABE16   gay/male/16

Beat. He types again.

ABE16   anyone out there?

Beat. He stares at the screen, waits.

A tympani roll accompanies a sharp blackout.

END OF PLAY

STEPHEN KARAM's plays include *The Humans* (Tony Award, Drama Critics Circle Award, Obie Award for Playwriting, and Pulitzer Prize finalist), *Sons of the Prophet* (Drama Critics Circle Award, Pulitzer Prize finalist), and *Speech & Debate*. His adaptation of Chekhov's *The Cherry Orchard* premiered on Broadway for the Roundabout Theatre Company.